AUTUMN REFLECTIONS

AUTUMN REFLECTIONS

Joan Copeland

Printed and bound in the UK by Aspect Design,
89 Newtown Road, Malvern, Worcs. WR14 1PD
Tel: 01684 561567
E-mail: allan@aspect-design.net
Website: www.aspect-design.net

ISBN 978-1-908832-86-3

Also by Joan Copeland
A Pocketful of Prayers

For CHRIS

my husband, lover, friend and fellow pilgrim for 50 years.

AUTUMN GOLD

Golden flecks in rocky ore amid Kent's gold hopyards,
hard rock smashed away,
sifted by suffering and adversity,
smelted by searing heat in meeting people's needs,
bright shining gold of Holy Spirit fire.

Moulding the molten stream through practice of ministry,
polishing over years of patient toil,
reflecting on God's work throughout our lives,
enriched by family joy, friendship
and seeing fruit from seeds planted years before.

Ourselves coming together,
friction wears off the dross,
intertwined strands of gold,
melting into each other, being one,
together we glorify our Lord.

Contents

JESUS and COMPANY

'I have called you friends.'

John 15 v.15

THE FIRSTBORN

Pharoah's firstborn son was slain.
All firstborn had to die.
The Hebrew doorposts daubed with blood
meant death would pass them by.
Did God kill them to save his own?
To let his people go?
Did blood of that Passover lamb
his wrath and anger show?

Another firstborn son was slain
when all deserved to die.
The lamb's blood staining wooden cross
meant pardon from on high.
Did God demand the sacrifice?
Father let this cup go!
Yet not my will but thine be done
that all your love might know.

GOD IMMANENT

Jacob saw the ladder set up to heaven from earth,
with angels going up and down all filled with holy mirth,
yet God was not removed from him behind the clouds to hide,
for while he saw the vision his God stood at his side.

Jacob wrestled all the night with stranger face to face.
He would not let him go until he blessed him with his grace.
The angel of the Lord smote him just at the break of day
so Jacob, though a blessing gained, went limping on his way.

John was in the spirit upon the Lord's own day.
He saw one like a son of man who shone like sun's bright ray.
As dead he fell before the Lord but, stretching out his hand,
the risen Christ took hold of him and gently bade him stand.

Not a distant God remote but one who stands beside us now,
who stretches his right hand to lift us up, himself does bow,
who by his presence gives us wounds as he did not come scatheless through
encounter with the Father's love but bears the scars of what we do.

MARY'S JOY

Mary's joy was that she knew
the secret true for everyone,
however difficult their lot
or problems were to overcome,
that in their 'fiat', 'Let it be
according to thy will',
the burden from their back would lift
and all surrendered be.

Her joy to look on other folk,
the folk she met in home or street,
and know that God was their Lord too,
in his hand all their lives and fears.
Only one thing needful was
their 'Yes' in penitence and tears,
and transformation of their years
would to his glory follow.

So with great joy did she set out
with Joseph, bound for Bethlehem,
knowing that, safe in Father's hands,
their whole time there was planned for them.
But how she longed to share her heart
with those who watched them setting forth,
some of her trust to them impart
in confidence of baby's birth.

'Jesus is Lord' we often say
yet we betray it with our lives,
our words, as we regard our friends
in whose lives he does not hold sway.
But Mary knew, in perfect trust,
though author of her own disgrace,
that given 'Yes', our Lord can bring
glory from shame in his embrace.

JOSEPH'S CRADLE

Well, man's or God's, he's got to have a cradle.
You can't shove a baby into any old box.
Whatever Mary says, and that's as maybe,
it's me and her will have to take the knocks.
> Mind you, I trust her. There's no girl like my Mary.
> Anyone would trust her with a babe new born.
> And that's what she's having, though she never knew the father,
> so I'll make him a cradle with these planks new sawn.
>> When she told me about it she said she'd seen an angel.
>> Well I've never seen one, leastways not here about.
>> But Mary said she'd seen him and God was the Father.
>> 'The baby is the Lord's' she said, 'without any doubt.'
It's no use thinking the folks here'll believe it.
It's me who'll get the blame, as Mary's a good lass,
So I'd better set to now and make the babe a cradle.
Do what I can to get her out of this mess.
> If he's God's baby, it'll have to be the finest,
> the best and finest cradle that's ever been made.
> I'll make it in a box shape, like I make the mangers,
> then put on little rockers, and for his head a shade.
>> I'll carve the sides with creatures, flowers and fishes,
>> surround him with the things that his Father made with love.
>> Here I'll put some lambkins, and oxen and a donkey,
>> there some trees and birds and a hovering dove.
>> I'll make a little scene with the reapers and the harvest,
>> with full ears of wheat and the bread that Mary bakes.
>> Then I'll carve a vineyard, with the pruners and the pickers,
>> a cluster of the fruit and the wine that it makes.
It was a lovely cradle, so lovingly fashioned
by the hand of Joseph for God's own Son,
but never did he use it, that dear little baby,
for he wasn't to be born in Nazareth town.
> In Bethlehem's city there was no room but a stable,
> no cradle but a manger full of hay and straw.
> Then to Egypt, fleeing from cruel King Herod.
> The cradle made for him other babies bore.
>> God's son? Man's son? Joseph made the cradle.
>> Made for the Son of God, his own sons served.
>> Man's sin? God's sin? Jesus took the punishment
>> upon a cruel wooden bed we all deserved.

'HE WILL BAPTISE...'

John the son of Zechariah
in the desert preached, 'Repent'.
People questioned in their minds,
'Was this one whom God had sent?'
> Jesus comes, the true Messiah,
> with the Spirit and with fire.

'Twas with water John baptised
for remission of their sin.
He who comes will come with fire,
let the Holy Spirit in.
> Jesus comes, the true Messiah,
> with the Spirit and with fire.

Jesus came to be baptised,
sharing our humanity.
God then sent his Spirit down,
showing his divinity.
> Jesus comes, the true Messiah,
> with the Spirit and with fire.

THE TEMPTATION

Jesus, when the devil listed
scriptures that were tried and tested,
with God's word you still resisted.
Let God's word still be our sword.

'If you are God's only Son,
make bread from this desert stone.'
'Shall man live by bread alone?'
Jesus answered with God's word.

Jesus, filled by Holy Spirit,
told he could the earth inherit,
said obedience had more merit.
He would worship God the Lord.

'Jesus, let God's angels guard you.
Throw yourself down – they will catch you.'
Jesus answered then, 'How read you?
Do not tempt the Lord your God.'

When we feel the tempter near us
whisp'ring words that would ensnare us,
Jesus, tempted Saviour, hear us.
Let your word still be our sword.

GOOD NEWS
Luke 4 v.18-19

He comes to preach the good news to the poor
to free them from the burden of the law
but those who, keeping rules are satisfied,
are deafened by their selfish pride.
      Good News! Good News! Is it Good News for you?
      Will you let Jesus do what you can't do?

He comes to claim release for those in chains,
give them true freedom out of all their pains,
but those who say, 'We are already free'
captive for ever in themselves will be.
      Good News! Good News! Is it Good News for you?
      Will you let Jesus do what you can't do?

He comes to let the blind receive their sight,
into their darkness shine his glorious light,
but those who say with confidence, 'We see'
cannot receive their light from me.
      Good News! Good News! Is it Good News for you?
      Will you let Jesus do what you can't do?

He comes to heal the deaf and let the dumb
shout out aloud and make the lame to run
but those who are not hampered in this way
will not rejoice at what he has to say.
      Good News! Good News! Is it Good News for you?
      Will you let Jesus do what you can't do?

THE BACKWARD LOT

Their leader a carpenter;
His best friends were fishermen,
rather smelly fishermen
hauling in their catch,
mending their nets
on the shores of Galilee.

Matthew, a tax-gatherer.
Ah yes, he was good with figures, was Matt.
Not very popular though
with those he taxed.

Simon Zelotes, yes,
one of those political demonstrators,
student riots, Scottish Nationalists,
a real firebrand was Simon.

Thomas, the doubter,
nice chap, Tom, but a bit slow,
had to have things spelt out to him, like.

What a bunch!
Put them in a classroom
and label them 'the backward lot'.
And yet... And yet...

Maybe the most brilliant men
the world has known
have served that carpenter.
Those fishermen were they
who turned the world upside down.

And I am proud
to serve that carpenter today.

UPS AND DOWNS
Matthew 14 v.13-33

We were all very low.
Already exhausted, worn out with constant crowds,
comings and goings, excitements.

That morning came the news;
John had been beheaded by Herod;
inevitable, I suppose, but it brought us very low.

We had been John's disciples.
John it was who introduced us.
Now he was dead.

And Jesus?
It must be hard for him. Cousins they were;
they had shared boyhood games, bar mitzvah, Passover.
Then when John appeared, Elijah in the wilderness,
he recognised the messenger, herald of his own coming.
Recognised by John as he baptised him.
Now John was dead.
What did that say of him, of his own mission?
We were very low.

'Come on, Lads, let's go!
Grab your things, the boat. We need a break.'
We did! Just what we needed,
just a few days camping in the hills,
just him and us, the twelve.

Calming it was, rowing across the sea,
sun glittering on the water, mountains above, blue sky;
it put things in perspective;
mountains, sea, wind and sky, birth, life and death
took their right place.

Then on the beach the crowds, waiting for us.
How our hearts sank!
It really was too much.

Only a few days peace and quiet...
Now here they were;
mothers with screaming kids, the sick and smelly,
pushing and shoving, arguing who was first.
Too bad!

He could have said, 'No'.
We could have gone round the lake or scarpered in the hills.

Not him! He really cared.
He felt for them, wanted to fill their needs.
Teaching and healing all that day.
We, with bad grace, trying to keep some order.

Then night came. Sun was setting.
'Send them home now. We've had all we can take.
Get rid of them. Surely we've earned our break?'

'They're hungry. Feed them.'
'Are you joking, Lord?
We packed in such a hurry, all we've got
is two small fish, five loaves.
That won't go far.'
'Bring them to me.'
We did. And then the miracle;
He took, and blessed, and broke; We gave them to the crowds
and kept on giving, giving, till we'd fed five thousand.
Tired we were, but what a high!
Feeding five thousand in the wilderness.
Now they would make him King.

But no!
'Back in the boat, Lads, now, and go across. I'll join you soon.'
Then disappeared, just went, into the hills to pray.

And we? We rowed across, but different now.
No sun, a sudden wind and gathering clouds,
waves rising, decks awash, swamping the boat.
It seemed like hours we rowed.
The storm was at its height when suddenly we saw him.

Surely not?
Must be a ghost walking upon the sea.
'Cheer up, Lads, it is I. Don't be afraid.'
Were we all scared!

Before I thought, I opened my big mouth,
'If it is you, Lord, bid me come to you
to prove you're not a ghost.'
'Come on!' he said.
Again, before I thought, I leapt down from the boat
and started out, walking upon the sea.
Walking upon the sea? On waves and wind?
How stupid can you get?
And then I sank.
'Help, Lord! Save me!' I cried.
'Why did you doubt?' he asked,
clasping me by the hand.
'Trust me!'

And then, and this I'll not forget,
Together, hand in hand, we walked back to the boat.
Just him and me.
And when we got aboard the sea was calm,
the wind had dropped, and we were safe.

A day of ups and downs, of highs and lows, of faith and doubt,
But never I'll forget
Together, hand in hand, we walked back to the boat,
Just him and me.

BELOVED DISCIPLE

I cannot bear to be loved.
I long for your approval, yes,
but that you should love me
on such a short acquaintance,
love me for myself and not my virtues:
that is too much.
I cannot take it in. I can't. I can't.
Your love breaks down my worth,
my estimated value in your eyes.
You don't approve of me:
You love me. I am lost.

Jesus had one disciple called beloved.
Was that because he loved him specially?
Or was the answer simpler?
That he alone, of all the twelve,
knew that the only reason he was there,
and that sufficient, was that he was loved.

Peter must have thought, and Judas certainly,
that Jesus needed just such men as they.
Approvingly he called them to his band.
Even doubting Thomas thought he could
win approbation dying with his Lord.

Maybe only John
accepted he was loved.
That was enough.

MARTHA AND MARY
Luke 10 v.38-42

Do come in. You must have a cup of tea.
I'll get out the china tea service,
knock up some scones and find the strawberry jam.
That tablecloth won't do. I'll iron the best.
Now everything is ready. You must go?
How disappointing, dear, we've had no time.
Do come again and let me know next time
so that I can prepare a proper tea.

Come in. I'm in a mess but do come in.
Let's both sit down.
Now tell me all your news and how you feel.
We'll share our views
and have a laugh or cry together.
You must go? I've not made a cup of tea
but it's been good, enjoying company.

'MARY STAYED IN THE HOUSE'

John 11 v.20, 2 Corinthians 12 v.7-10

Mary: How can I face my Lord, life-giving, healing one?
Now lies my brother dead.
If he had come… Or if we'd had more faith…
he'd not have died.
How can I face my Lord
with that denial of his living power
shaming me in my brother's death?

Joan: How can I face my Lord, life-giving, healing one,
as I lie here in bed?
If more had prayed… Or if I'd had more faith…
I would be well.
How can I face my Lord
with that denial of his living power
shaming me in my disability?

Paul: How can I face my Lord, life-giving, healing one
with this thorn in the flesh?
I prayed three times… I exercised my faith…
It still remained.
But I can face my Lord
with affirmation of his living power,
his glory in my very weakness shown.

THE PRODIGAL SON

Out of all the nations upon earth
God chose just one.
Abraham's seed, the Israelites,
to be his chosen nation, his own son.
Conscious of this relationship,
they served their God with awe.
With him as their protector, covenanted
to be his chosen people, keep his law.
Throughout the ages they were separate,
scorning the gods of nations round about,
on pain of death preserved their purity,
loving their brethren, keeping strangers out.

Another Son the Father had, who came and loved and gave
of all his Father's riches to poor and sick and slave,
identified himself with sin, suffered and hungered sore.
Punished for prodigality, rewarded for the ills he bore.

But when the prodigal returned,
the perfect penitent, to be forgiven,
the Father welcomed him with open arms,
the Messianic feast prepared in Heaven.
The prodigal rejoiced with friends,
the ones who'd shared his cup on earth.
The sinners, by his love forgiven,
sat down and shared the feast with mirth.

While Abraham's seed, the righteous ones,
who'd served their God so faithfully,
looked on with jealous eyes and hearts,
complaining loud and bitterly
that Father should take back the Son
who'd spent his riches, broke the law,
admitted sinners to the place
reserved and earned by them before.

'YOU DID IT UNTO ME'

'Inasmuch as you have done it to the least of these,
you did it unto me.'
So you said, Lord.
How often have we thought,
as we some action for another took,
we did it unto thee.
How that thought warmed our heart,
as we felt sure
that gratitude from you was quite enough
for what we did.

But to receive on your behalf, dear Lord,
is quite another thing.
You promised no reward for that.
That we should bear your gracious part,
imitate your humble heart,
helpless become, that others might
serve you in us, for their reward.

MARY

Overwrought and drained,
her love snatched from her
in those brief few days.
Yet she must do something.
Blindly, unknowingly, she blundered forth,
creeping to the dawn-dark garden.
Four blank walls enclosing her
and her own body blocked the entrance,
excluding all the light.
Four blank walls.
He wasn't there.
Terror. Blind panic. Help!
What to do? Which way to go?
Confronted with four blank walls,
benumbed, she stumbled out,
unseeing, into the dawn-bright garden,
tear-blinded, despair-haunted.
What? Where? Why?

'Mary' he said.
Her love arose,
sun shone,
and all is well.

EASTER JOY AND GRIEF

'Then were the disciples glad when they saw the Lord.'
John 20 v.20

Yes, we were glad, and overjoyed, amazed
that Jesus was alive. With grief we had been crazed.
But still we grieved for certainties we'd known
when he was always with us, moving from home to home.

We'd seen him heal, teach crowds and calm the sea.
Adventures every day; the lame run, blind men see.
Beneath the stars at night, if we woke, he was not there.
Yet even then we knew he'd be in the hills at prayer.

Now from death he's risen but, though we know he lives,
we're never sure when he'll appear. Disturbing peace he gives.
Old certainties have gone, dispelled by Easter light.
We learn to live a different way, walking by faith, not sight.

THE VISION

Saul had a vision, Lord Jesus, of thee
in risen light blinding, so he could not see.
In Christians he'd fought thee and thrown into jail.
No human could change him, but you could not fail

We, who would serve thee by doing thy will,
love others for thy sake, not wishing them ill,
to us comes no vision to turn us around,
no voices and lightning throw us to the ground.

'Child', you say gently, 'you know you are mine.
You pray to me daily and know I am thine.
Your faith is most blessed, for you have not seen
and yet have believed me, obeyed the unseen.'

In life everlasting the saints shall be one;
the sinners converted like prodigal son;
the ones who have served thee both faithful and long;
all shall see the vision and praise thee in song.

COLOSSIANS ch.1 v.15-20 1980s STYLE

God, whom we cannot see, we see in him;
God in a mirror, reflection come alive.

He is ace, the tops, the one in charge.
The powers that be, the government,
the laws of nature, atoms, nuclear power,
He heads them all.
They were his bright idea,
He holds the master key, programmes each one.
He's mastermind, the one who knows,
the managing director, the Big Boss, JC.

He's the One who planned the rescue bid.
When all was lost, floated the company,
revalued shares,
revamped the image,
which we all reflect.

PEOPLE AND PLACES

'The Lord is good to all,
and his compassion is over all that he has made.'

Psalm 145 v.9

DRESSING PRAYER for OAPs

In the name of the Father and of the Son and of the Holy Spirit.
I put my face cream on in shape of cross,
praying for your protection through the day.
My denture next I fix with thankful praise
for food and drink providing daily need.
As I insert an aid into each ear,
open my ears that I may hear your voice.
As I put on my specs, open my eyes
that I may see Jesus in the folk I meet.
My watch goes on – my time is yours today.
My cross reminds me of your constant presence.
And as I take my stick, give me support
to live this day unto your glory, Lord.

RETIRED?

Retirement now is bad for you!
Official. On the news.
By all means have a few weeks off,
a holiday, a cruise.

But after that it's back to work.
The benefits are fine:
a social network, exercise,
a way to pass the time.

'There are no jobs', I hear you cry.
No problem. Volunteer!
Lyttelton Well will welcome you
with open arms, no fear.

Whether the bookshop, office work,
café or pastoral care,
maintenance of buildings, kitchen help,
washing tea towels, or prayer.

WE NEED YOU!

NOT YET...

A prayer and healing service did you say?
I'd love to come but not just right away.
I've just got this new job, a responsible position.
I must be on my toes. There's a lot of competition.

I'll wait until the children are grown up and off my hands.
It's amazing how one's teenagers make so many demands.
Not that I try to swamp them with too much care and love,
but one has to organise them, and sometimes give a shove.

I must reserve my failing strength for things that really count,
and of spare time for other things I have a small amount.
When I have sorted out my life, and proved that I can cope,
then I'll have time to come and pray for faith and love and hope.

'I'M GOING TO LIVE FOR EVER!'

'I'm going to live for ever!' with force she did declare,
stifling a little groan on rising from her chair.
She'd taken all her vitamins, anti-wrinkled face and neck,
attended her keep-fit class and walked around the deck.

One of many passengers enjoying a sea cruise
but fervently denying that they were bound to lose
their health and looks and faculties, eventually die.
We all must share in the pretence and help to live the lie.

'I'm going to live for ever!' 'You're right, and so am I,
but not in this life,' I replied, 'with Jesus when I die!'

FORETASTE OF HEAVEN
for Sandy and Liz

At last we have arrived
after meandering through the Worcester lanes;
ever decreasing circles, next left turn.

You stand at open door,
welcome each one into your home,
a smile of recognition, friendly word;
we enter in.

Spacious and ordered, homely and relaxed,
and filled with light,
coloured with bowls of flowers,
views across lawns and trees.
We settle with the Lord
in fellowship.

And as we pray
your gentle words of knowledge,
wisdom and prophecy affirm each one.
We are encouraged in our pilgrimage.

Then generously you serve
the meal you have prepared, as Jesus did.
We sit together, share a family meal.
You bless us on our way
as we go out into God's needy world,
refreshed to do his will.
Thank you.

HUG IN PERSON

How good it is, as we live out our lives,
to meet so many and such varied folk,
becoming friends, sharing our thoughts and words,
experience of heady youth, raising our children,
becoming middle aged,
sorrows and joys of growing old.

How good it is to keep in touch by letter or by phone,
and now email and skype, exchanging news
at Christmas, birthday cards,
remembering them in prayer.

All these are good but as the years go by
I am convinced that nothing can replace
a hug in person. Such hugs say it all.
Worth all the effort, travel, tiredness, time,
to visit friends, be with them in the flesh.
So was the Incarnation:
Jesus, God's hug in Person,
to our world, to each of us
with love.

THE LOOP

'Child, listen for my whisper.' Desmond Tutu

I wear two hearing aids.
They're such a help
and, when I tune in to the loop,
I hear only what is said into the microphone
and nothing else.

Teach me to listen for your whisper, Lord,
to tune in to your loop
and hear your voice.

SEPARATION

'Two will become one flesh.'
So we became over the years
entwined in body, thought and deed,
one flesh.
Then ripped apart.
My other half, part of myself, is gone.
God, why?
God, why have you done this to me?
Pain. Horror. Void. Black hole.
My other half has died.

The Son, who from eternity had been
one with the Father,
perfect Unity, one God.
Then ripped apart.
Made to be sin who knew no sin.
God, why?
God, why have you forsaken me?
Pain. Horror. Void. Black hole.
The Son surrendered.
Died.

NEW LEGS FOR OLD?

'Where can I get two new legs?'
she asked at the church door.
'In heaven we'll all be made new;
new bodies and much more.'

'Christ has died and Christ is risen'
each week we proclaim.
The resurrection of our bodies
we believe the same.

Our outer body wears away,
said Paul, just to prepare
us for a weight of glory
which is quite beyond compare.

An earthly body it is sown,
but it will surely rise
a heavenly body, quite renewed,
ascending to the skies.

So when we lose our health and strength
by bodies wearing out,
let us look forward, celebrate,
laugh and sing and shout,

That when we put aside our tent
which served us well on earth,
a new, strong, vigorous beauty
will be ours by heavenly birth.

Because our Lord both died and rose
to demonstrate his love,
we all will rise in glory
to share his life above.

MEETING MARGARET

'A loop around your walking stick
with velcro fastening would be a help.'
As we sat at supper my heart leaped.
I'd found a friend, a fellow traveller,
with whom I felt completely at my ease
and loved on sight.

And while you chatted to another guest
of neonatal nursing, common experience,
I opened up your book with sheer delight
at drawings, poems, vivid pen portraits,
and was absorbed.

'Venice was fun,' you said.
And all of life, shining and smiling in your eyes
was good, to be enjoyed,
packed full of interest, colourful, vibrant,
filled with God's life, even the painful bits.

This gift was from the Lord;
although I knew that I was here
for all the guests,
I felt no sense of guilt at my delight,
sharing with you.

And now at home, your book a hidden joy
to which I turn for treasured tastes,
to deepen and a renew a friendship just begun
into eternal life.

WHITE STICK
for Daphne

I've been a carer all my life
but now I cannot see.
I'm not completely blind. I wonder
if that would easier be?

Voices I recognise, of course,
and friends still give me hugs,
but I can't read and faces are
vague pinkish talking blobs.

But mostly what I really miss
when I'm in a strange place
is seeing the expression
on the other person's face,
and reading body language
showing happiness or pain,
a stranger reaching out to me,
or glad to meet again.

Eye contact is not possible
across the dinner table.
Responding to disembodied sound,
I simply am not able.

They gave me a white stick, I thought,
to help me get around.
My pride forbade me using it,
but maybe now I've found
its purpose really is to tell
the ones I cannot see
that here is someone who needs help
and understanding. Me.

FEAR NOT
for Gabrielle

'I believe in God, who made me and all the world'
out of his love.
How could the love that gentles me
so kindly in the palm of his own hand
do me some harm?
Each part of me he made, and keeps, and heals.
Why then deny the final touch,
the work his Spirit seals?

'I believe in Jesus Christ, his Son'
who loved me, died and gave himself for me.
Yet even he was by the Spirit filled
to do all of the works the Father willed.
Without that power could not have healed the sick,
cleansed lepers, raised the dead or preached Good News.
So what he needed, and now offers me,
can I refuse?

'I believe in the Holy Spirit'
proceeding from the Father and the Son.
Shall he, who comes from those who love so much,
who made and saved my life, my mind, my soul,
do me some harm? How could that be?
Fear not my heart, and open to his knock,
the he may dwell within,
and I complete may be.

SIGNS OF HIS LOVE
for Penny

The one who prayed said, 'Look for signs
of God's love for you each day.
It may not be quite obvious, or that for which we pray,
        But you will know.'

Our daughter came for the weekend and, taking her for tea,
within the crowded car park was one space, just for me
and, once inside the crowded cafe, one table left, for three.
        I saw the sign.

Wheeled to the chapel in a chair, I looked for signs of God's love there:
The final tune the lullaby which I'd sung every night
to children as they went to sleep, protecting them from fright.
        Comforting sign.

My first chemo I'd dreaded but all day I was aware
of loving hands surrounding me as I nestled in his care.
I knew that I was God's dear child completely safe from harm.
That knowledge gave me confidence, kept me relaxed and calm.
        Sign of his love.

A 'hunt the thimble' every day as I look for the sign
of God's directed love to me, token of power divine.
Not instant healing miracles, but how much I have grown
in knowledge of his love for me, and that I am his own
        through signs of love.

WHAT WOULD JESUS DO?
for a lady who 'only cooks'

A little girl he raised to life
when she'd been lying dead.
What did he tell Mum and Dad?
'Give her some food,' he said.

Peter's mother-in-law was sick
and Jesus raised her up.
How did she show praise and thanks?
Invited them to sup.

Disciples, sad and at loose end,
go out all night to fish.
'Come to breakfast,' said the Lord,
'I've cooked a tasty dish.'

People suffering trauma
come to The House of Bread
for ministry by word and prayer,
and bodies too are fed.

This is incarnation,
spirit and body whole.
We give holistic ministry,
feed body, mind and soul.

Thank you that you show us,
by serving up a meal,
we minister your love, O Lord,
through food which makes grace real.

EXHIBITION
Sixty Seasons by David Nash

Fame, recognition,
individual exhibition.

'Do you have any of his work?'
Only one painting on the wall,
the box that he made, but I use that,
and the bunks, made by a friend
acting as jobbing carpenter.
Funny to think a friend is famous now.

How many folk in Nazareth's small town
had furniture made by a jobbing carpenter?
Was its value then 'made by a friend'?
Did it inflate when fame and miracles attached to him,
then notoriety of public execution?
How many still his friends
treasured wood shaped by hands
that made the world?

GOD'S ANTHOLOGY

In time the Lord will see us in his book:
the comic verse, the sonnet serious,
and he will laugh so richly to enjoy
the poetry for his enjoyment made.

The pantomime in rhyming couplets all,
in demon king portraying Adam's fall,
in fairy queen the power of goodness shown,
and humans all 'twixt good and evil blown.

A dirge, a requiem, a sad lament
cry from the heart humanity's sad lot;
a weeping by the foreign willow tree
for Paradise which we have ne'er forgot.

The graceful tripping of the roundelay,
the dancing measure of life's jollity,
laughter that sings and shouts, 'Hip hip hooray!'
The wine of celebration, Cana's feast.

The love song, sonnet, deep emotion's measure
words incomplete that mock our deep desires,
spilling at his dear feet our costliest treasure,
our highest loves, unquenched eternal fires.

So the great Author of our poetry
will bind us in the volume of his love,
and at his will take pleasure in us all,
reading our lives in his great home above.

THIN PLACES, THIN PEOPLE

Thin places there are on this earth,
as Jacob found at Bethel,
where suddenly we are aware
that God is here,
here in this place.
A glory moment.
Heaven touches earth,
and we are changed.

There are thin people too,
almost transparent.
As we look at them
and hear them speak,
we catch a glimpse of God
and hear his voice.
A glory moment.
God's love touches lives
and we are changed.

INTERCESSION

My friends ask me to pray for them
when they are in great need
but sometimes I don't have the words,
know how to intercede.

As, Lord, I bring dear ones to you
for comfort, strength and ease,
I carry them within my heart
where loving does not cease.

Jesus, my Lord, you ever live
to intercede for me.
You carry me within your heart
for all eternity.

Grant us the knowledge, dearest Lord,
that in your heart we dwell
in trouble, sorrow, fear and death,
and all things shall be well.

THE HAIRS ON YOUR HEAD

Your Father knows
how many hairs you have,
what colour and how long;
He counts them, every one,
so Jesus said.

As I sit on the bus,
I see the heads in front of me.
According to my hairdresser
each head of hair's unique.

How wonderful to think
that each and every person whom we meet
existed as a twinkle in God's eye
before the universe,
before Big Bang or evolution came to be,
because he loves.

So as I sit and look
at different heads of hair,
I pray for them
a blessing on each one.
Lord Jesus Christ have mercy
on driver, passengers,
and those they meet today.
Lord Jesus Christ, have mercy.

ENCOUNTER

A barge traversing locks.
Why is it, every time,
the woman clambers up,
the man stands still?
She turns the cogs,
strains at the bar,
and out he steers,
the captain of his craft.

The woman shouts,
asks if we're doing checks
on water level.
'No, writing poetry.'
'Come, share it then.'
I do. We stand and chat.
She comes from Mississip.
Now, by the Severn,
I offer her 'A Pocketful of Prayers'.
She shares her dream.
We part with mutual blessing.

MIND, BODY, SPIRIT

'Mind, body, spirit, which shelf is that?'
'We don't… Try Smiths or Beacon Books.'
When she had gone, and having thought,
well – every book we have should deal with that.

I sampled some. 'Why am I here?'
If I had asked why she was here it might have helped.
I searched the shelves in vain – I must conclude
that Christians write alone for Christians in the know.

If life is hard and you have never heard Good News,
why not ask here for 'Body, mind and spirit'?
That's where a Christian has to go in Smiths
or Waterstones to look for Bibles or theology.

May you, dear Lord, forgive our lack of sight.
Next time may we provide for body, mind and spirit
of those in need.

VALUE

EVENING MEAL
A day's hard work
picking the peas and shelling them,
onions and sage to chop,
breadcrumbs to rub, and cook
the meat bought from the shop.

ECONOMICS
My earnings for an hour
would buy the best in Tesco;
frozen veg, ready made sauce,
duck in red wine
and cheesecake for dessert.

STIPEND
Enough to live on
for a lifetime's work,
counted and paid for not in hours
but other people's lives,
their hopes and fears.
Worth in eternity.

MUM

You are the focus,
the centre of the gathered circle
of our loving concern.
    Noisily the ventilator breathes for you,
    pumping air into damaged lungs.
        Helplessly we gaze upon your face,
        willing your eyes to open, lips to smile,
        your voice to say, 'Dear, dear' as you return.
            We hold your hands
            that cooked and washed and cleaned,
            praying as we squeeze that they'll respond.
            The hands that made us dolls and woolly toys,
            knitted and sewed our clothes with loving care.
                You are the focus
                and the centre point of all our love,
                our desperate longing prayer.
Yet we, too, are the focus of your love,
closer together now than e'er before.
Aware of all your love has meant to us,
aware, too, of each other's love for you.
    Unselfish love you gave each one of us,
    seeking our good, praising our strengths,
    convicting us of wrong, forgiving weaknesses,
    with patience and compassion in your touch.
        Yet while you lived we took all you could give
        for our own strength.
        The focus of your love
        as you lay silent, still, drew us together,
        closer each to each, aware of others' needs,
        putting them first as you had done.
            Learning to pray and mean, 'Thy will be done.'
            Trusting the Lord to work all things for good,
            as you had done.
So you drew us into a family of greater love,
a silent focus of the love of God,
praising him in death as in your life.
    The Lord has given and he takes away.
    Blessed, blessed, blessed be his name.

written after my Mother's death in 1994

MEMORY

A battered leather case,
just large enough to hold some documents,
a photo of the squadron, D Flight, November '43,
the cap with RAF badge, crested eagle buttons;
uniform worn with pride.
My Dad's mementoes.

But I remember him, first memory,
standing at our front gate in a policeman's helmet.
Another uniform after he'd been demobbed,
and I a toddler.

Now he is dead,
and all his memories only mine
because I listened as he talked;
of service in Rhodesia;
a pilot who forgot the southern hemisphere
and died because he saw the sun in the wrong place;
of Capetown and the Table Mountain there;
how the troopship strained and curved
crossing the Bay of Biscay;
patrolling London's streets in blacked out night;
the swish of a swan's flight
mistaken for a parachute descending;
felt the fear.

And earlier memories;
Wolf Cubs and Scouts;
staged battles in dug out trenches
when a stone near killed one of his mates.

How glad I am I listened as we walked,
and I remember.

PINK PEARDROP

Pink peardrop
heady scent
invoking memories
of childhood.
My father's memories
of aircraft dope,
days in the R.A.F.
Tales that I listened to,
enthralled.
Remembered
in the smell
of pink peardrop.

...AND GIVE YOU PEACE

A splitting head; the G.P. comes,
an ambulance arrives.
Brain haemorrhage they think it is.
Not everyone survives.
> Around us both the storm blows fierce
> the waves are wild and steep.
> Upon a cushion in the stern Jesus lies fast asleep
> and we are safe with him.

All day in Worcester Royal; question after question;
test after test after test.
At length a bed, and late at night
to move him there is best.
> Around us both the storm blows fierce
> the waves are wild and steep.
> Upon a cushion in the stern Jesus lies fast asleep
> and we are safe with him.

A blue light job on motorways,
often the sirens sound.
Skilled driver, nurses in the back,
to Oxford we are bound.
> Around us both the storm blows fierce
> the waves are wild and steep.
> Upon a cushion in the stern Jesus lies fast asleep
> and we are safe with him.

An operation must be done
within the next two days,
but angiogram is broken down
so everybody prays.
> Around us both the storm blows fierce
> the waves are wild and steep.
> Upon a cushion in the stern Jesus lies fast asleep
> and we are safe with him.

Eventually on day six
machine is working fine.
Anaesthetist and medic team
stem trouble just in time.

> Around us both the storm blows fierce
> the waves are wild and steep.
> Upon a cushion in the stern Jesus lies fast asleep
> and we are safe with him.

Thanks be to God, and all our friends
who lifted us in prayer,
who hold us in his presence,
his healing and his care.

> Around us both the storm blows fierce
> the waves are wild and steep.
> Upon a cushion in the stern Jesus lies fast asleep
> and we are safe with him.

SOLUTION

My sister's leaving home party
launching her WRENS career.
My parents' cottage,
small, with two front rooms
divided by hall and stairs.

Village community.
My Mum befriended all,
quite indiscriminate,
but many there nursed ancient feuds,
their families didn't speak.
So what to do?

All were invited and all came.
The cutting of the cake was in the hall.
And those to whom your family didn't speak
were in the other room.

DOES GOD HAVE HOLES IN?

'Does God have holes in, Granny?'
Lauren asked.
'Does God have holes in?'
while we made mince pies,
remembering Bethlehem
and God made man,
the Baby in the manger,
Jesus Christ.
Does God have holes?

Indeed he does,
for that dear Babe was pierced
through hands and feet and side
upon the cross,
and still he bears
those tokens of his passion, glorified,
which angels wonder at and we adore.
Yes, God has holes.

And we who follow him
take up our cross,
receive our share of wounds,
will share his scars.
We too have holes.

WAITING FOR THE QUEEN

THE FLAG

Made to be waved,
waved once, then thrown away.
In China made, of course,
I happened to be stamped red, white and blue.
Oblong of plastic with a plastic stalk.
Disposable.
Yet I can play a part.
The little boy, excited, grips me hard
and with my clone grasped in his other hand
he waves us both,
smiles for the photographer:
a captured moment in the waiting game.

Later on I'll be waved
to sound of shouting as a car sweeps past.
A lady in a hat will also wave,
but a gloved hand, to cheering waving crowds.
Then I'll be thrown away,
trashed in the landfill site,
but caught for ever in the photograph.
A precious memory.

WAITING

My Mummy said, 'We're going to see the Queen.'
She's so excited at the treat in store.
My Granny's coming too. So here we are.
    What are we waiting for?

    Granny tells me funny little rhymes
    about a Queen and mouse upon the floor
    under her chair with diamonds big as shoes.
        Is that what we're waiting for?

        So many people here. They're pushing us
        against the railings. Rain begins to pour,
        then sun comes out again, and still we wait.
            What are we waiting for?

            I sit on Granny's lap on wobbly stool.
            Her knees are knobbly and my bottom's sore.
            The man then takes a photo which is fun,
                but what are we waiting for?

                We've waited here two hours, then suddenly
                the crowd begins to roar. A car drives past
                with lady in a hat. Was that the Queen?
                    Was that what we waited for?

HELP! HELP!

'Help! Help!' cries little Henry, raising hands
against the smooth straight trunk of a great pine,
quite certain that his loving Granny will,
somehow, triumphantly, help him to gain
access to topmost branch.

'Help! Help!' we cry to God when faced with needs
both of our own and those of all our friends.
Our faith is not as sure as Henry's is
but, as we pray, I hear the sound of chainsaw.
God's own plan might be to fell the tree
so that we, easily, may walk along the trunk
to topmost branch.

RELATIONSHIP

Family Christmas: daughter, already stressed from work,
ensuring each of us enjoyed ourselves.
We all had a good time.
On the last day, she and I sat down
over a cup of tea for a good chat.
At that point my husband said it was time to go.
    Then, in my rage, I realized I was lonely,
      never spent time over a cup of coffee with a friend
      or daughter, chatting of this or that,
        being,
          face to face,
            building relationship.

After Christmas, quite without intent, I hurt a friend.
Forgiveness asked and given.
Then I found a poem she'd sent me
on friendship forty years ago.
    Again I realised I'd not spent recent time with her alone,
      just sitting, chatting, listening, keeping close,
        being,
          face to face,
            keeping relationship.

Communication, instant, all pervasive
on mobile, email, facebook, internet,
the constant chatter of a myriad voices,
insulating us, as do our cars, from other selves,
barring communion.
    How many lonely folk, lacking all human contact,
    travel on buses, shop in the supermart
    in order to exchange a word or two
    with someone face to face.
      A person who'll sit beside them on the bus,
      listen to details of their daily lives,
      chatting together, briefly, fleetingly,
        being,
          face to face,
            precious relationship.

WYCHALL LANE CHURCH

They have the answers, Lord,
it's all sewn up.
Six hundred come to Sunday Services.
The house church with its hundred members,
all 'born again' and Spirit filled of course,
are all completing Bible questionnaires.
There's much that we can learn
from management techniques,
and use of group dynamics in the church.

So when I think of 'our lot', Lord,
our tatty band, the jobless and the poor,
the ones who cannot cope with life,
or those who cope by sin,
it nearly breaks my heart.
How do we teach them, Lord?
Those who can barely read,
or make sure, as they start the Christian life,
they jump through the right hoops?
They only have their need.
We only have your love.

A silver cross against the midnight blue
of sorrows manifest, yet hidden from the world.

I look, Lord, at your cross and think of you.
You came and loved and gave.
You lived among the poor and prostitutes,
the refuse and the dregs of humankind.
You healed them, loved and cared,
with no support,
and at the end you died
alone.
Not a success.
Nor are we, Lord.
Teach us to be content
to follow you.

'CREATIVE DAY'

The folk at church were good to me
when I was pretty low,
and as they loved and cared for me
the Lord I came to know.
      Praise the Lord!

One day they said, 'Why don't you come
on a Creative Day?'
I'd no idea just what that was,
but joined in anyway.
      Praise the Lord!

Well there were paintings, flowers and dance,
puppets and drama too,
and workshops which we all joined in,
my friends and, yes, me too.
      Praise the Lord!

I'm middle aged and overweight,
and stiff in hips and knees.
'Just praise the Lord in dance' she said,
'Imagine you're a breeze.'
      Praise the Lord!

I focused on the Lord and danced
for him who'd made me 'me',
and as I danced for his delight
I knew he'd set me free
      Praise the Lord!

'Lord of the Dance' we sing to him,
and that I day I found out
I too could praise the Lord in dance,
and play and sing and shout,
      'Praise the Lord!'

THE VICAR AND HIS WIFE

CHRIS   The vicar should be very good at making conversation,
         mouthing polite enquiries on the health of each relation.
         I ask them if they're Christians, if they believe in God,
         but people take offence at that and think me very odd.
         'Religion is our own affair, and no one has the right
         to ask us questions of that sort.' I give them quite a fright.
                 How very ill-mannered of the vicar!

JOAN   China teacups, silver pots are what the folks expect to see,
         cucumber sandwiches and cakes at the vicarage for tea.
         My coffee's served in half pint mugs, the bread's not sliced too thin;
         spaghetti bolognese is fun and dribbles down your chin.
         We've no starched linen tablecloths, the jam's still in a jar,
         and as for sugar tongs and such, we don't know what they are.
                 The vicar's wife! Just fancy!

CHRIS   Saint Francis preached to all the birds. He was a holy man.
         To me the pigeons are a pest. I'll get them if I can.
         They're in the tower, they block the drains and make the church roof leak,
         then when I've put in all my plants, my cabbages they tweak.
         I asked my friend to come and help with accurate air gun.
         He had a go and hit the foe, and shot them every one.
                 How dreadful! Encouraged by the vicar!

JOAN   'The Mothers' Union was run by our first vicar's wife.
         She led the meetings beautifully and calmed the slightest strife.'
         But having been to college with a lot of jolly men
         I simply can't stand meetings that would suit a clucking hen.
         I'd rather have an argument, be letting down my hair,
         than smile at them all sweetly, graciously take the chair.
                 Dear dear! And she's the vicar's wife!

CHRIS   'Vicar, the bolt's come off the door, the toilet door' (face red)
        'with all those people using it, it must be put right,' she said.
        'I quite agree. I'm sure you have screwdrivers.' I replied,
        and waited then to see results from the pressure I'd applied.
        I waited for three solid months through many more complaints
        until one of the P.C.C. came to the aid of needy saints.
                But really it should have been the vicar!

JOAN   Of course my happy family should be neat, clean and polite.
        Instead my elder daughters take an unholy delight
        in shouting at the Wolf Cubs as they walk on the church wall,
        and if they cannot tip them off, in hoping that they'll fall.
        Meanwhile the youngest shocks the church by yelling for her potty
        in the middle of Dad's sermon, and exposing her bare botty.
                The vicar's wife should be a model mother!

BOTH   We don't live up to expectations, and yet we both well know
        that when we've finished our work here and it's time for us to go,

JOAN   The ladies of the parish will declaim with tearful fuss,
        'You're just not like the vicar's wife. You're more like one of us.'

CHRIS   And all the congregation say, eyes weeping not a few,
        'You've not been like a vicar here. You're really human too.'

THERE IS A PLACE

There is a place
beyond the Valley of the Rocks,
past the White Lady, over all the humps.
There is a place.
    Lee Abbey, set in fields
    above the cliffs and bay,
    facing the sea, God's welcome.
    There is a place.
        And there, there is a special place
        for each and every guest
        where they can hear God say, 'Just talk to Me.'
        There is a place.
            My room, the welcome smiles when I arrive,
            view from the window,
            bed for much needed sleep
            where I can rest safe in my Father's arms.
            There is a place.
                The dining room, refreshment, nourishment,
                chocolates in Lent and wine by candlelight,
                shared with the family of God,
                a foretaste of the heavenly feast
                where we will be the bride.
                There is a place.
The Octag where I glimpse
the glory of the worship of the heavens,
the saints in company with angel host
praising the King of heaven.
There is a place.
    Small Lounge, cosy and homelike,
    where the peace envelopes those who pray
    and meditate, bringing to God the world
    in newspapers and word of mouth,
    the world for which he died.
    There is a place.
        The chapel, upper room, silent and empty,
        light focussed on the cross, the holy place
        where I can hear your voice addressed to me.
        There is a place.

Outside on the estate a multitude of places,
each one special for the special one
who speaks to you and hears your voice.
There is a place.

    The seat where I can sit
    watching the sheep sleepily chewing grass,
    the lambs at play,
    remember the Good Shepherd and the Lamb of God.
    There is a place.

        The walk to Jenny's Leap
        inviting me along the way of God,
        life's journey beckoning in him who is the Way.
        There is a place.

            The clifftop, gazing down
            at rocks and waves breaking in clouds of spray,
            seagulls beneath me riding on the wind.
            How great thou art in thy creation, Lord.
            There is a place.

                I scramble down the path
                and seat myself upon a slab of rock.
                There I can hear you speak,
                rest in security. You are my Rock.
                There is a place.

We climb the hill together till we come
to three tall crosses stark against the sky
and wonder yet again that God should love
so much and send his Son to die.
There is a place.

    A clearing in the woods
    from which I see the house, home of community,
    the family of which we are a part,
    and know the joy of our true home
    after our earthly pilgrimage is done
    where we shall live for all eternity in fellowship.
    There is a place.

LEE ABBEY COMMUNITY

I came with such ideals
to be a member of community
here at Lee Abbey in the Devon hills,
the perfect house with perfect views.
And I would be a beacon of your love,
sharing my faith with those who came,
blessing them in your name.

But the reality!
A heavy round of stripping beds
and making them again,
collecting rubbish and lost property.
And if another guest asks where
I come from and how long I've been
here on community,
I'll scream.
Lord, did I get it wrong?

The Lord says, 'My reality is richer still.
You cannot see while you are here
how I transform your offering
of hard and heavy work,
the steaming kitchen's noise and heat,
the welcoming of guests
when you are tired or cross.
But by your offering made once, and every day,
by will, not inclination, the guests are blessed.

I see them journey here, tired, stressed and ill.
You welcome them
and, soaked in prayer and offered lives,
Lee Abbey brings my peace into their lives.
They are surprised by welcome.
Then quite gradually your loving care,
the beauty and the prayer
enfolds them in my love and they are healed.
I see them as they leave. Their lives are changed
and they can live in me because of you.'

DAVE HOPWOOD

Dave, miming creator God,
imagines universe,
breathes out the stars,
fashions the details,
cares for straying lambs,
and all in love
to draw us into Love.

Dave, on breakfast team,
surveys the guests,
frowning in concentration,
then observes,
takes necessary action,
provides for needs,
reflects the love of God.

GOOD FRIDAY 2014 – AT THE CROSSES

'Eleven till twelve noon', the programme states,
'Reflection at the Crosses'.
We discuss over the meal how we get there;
very steep up the meadow to the top;
a longer path with gentler slope is possible;
or the Land Rover – getting in's a problem and it shakes up your bones.
'But when we get there, will there be chairs to sit on?'
We would prefer an armchair seat to watch Christ die.

We walk slowly up the hill, chatting of this and that.
When we arrive we sit on sunlit turf or stand around,
a goodly crowd of more than fifty folk.
Three empty crosses stand against a pure blue sky,
beneath them four Roman soldiers play at dice,
hammer in nails and sit around their fire.
We wait.   And nothing happens.
The soldiers walk to the crosses, play at dice again.
We wait.   And nothing happens.
The time is long, the time it takes to die.
We wait.   And nothing happens.
Some of us realise then – nothing will happen.
No drama now like that we shared last night.
No passion play.
We wait.   And nothing happens.
Slowly we wander off in twos and threes,
get back while coffee still is being served.
Crowd thins to half a dozen who wait still.
                           And nothing happens.
The soldiers all pack up, go down the hill.
                           And nothing happens.
Three empty crosses stand against the still blue sky,
as we all leave,
leave Jesus hanging still,
taking so long to die for our salvation.

WORCESTER CATHEDRAL
or ENERGY

Thousands at its beginning
investing many years
the footprint, effort, cost,
until it stands
to give to needy souls
in different kind.

Now, giving to those who come
in search of entertainment,
not in need,
we measure what is given
as shelter, warmth and light
in carbon footprint cost.

Ignoring at the centre,
burning, clear and still,
fount of all energy,
creation's source.

SAINT GEORGE'S CHAPEL

Saint George's Chapel, where I came to write
memories of my father, prompted by the theme of hats.
On the prayer desk his RAF cap lies
with photo of his squadron.
In the stained glass window others in uniform;
A nurse in headdress, white, a sailor holds his cap,
a pilot his helmet and a soldier in tin hat,
protected by a knight of former times in iron casque.
Surmounted by the king from Revelation in gold coronet,
Jesus depicted with a halo bright.
Yet nowhere in this window, in praise of those who died,
is crown of thorns.
I look again.
There, beneath St George's feet,
the dragon's head, are thorns,
sharp thorns, on twisted brambles green,
now conquered.

SAINT JOHN'S CHAPEL, WORCESTER CATHEDRAL

Empty space now:
nine chairs against the walls, and three prie-dieux,
an altar here, clearly unused,
with painted reredos, bright crucifixion scene.

Empty, but not unused.
At the west end a door, 'Private, staff only',
bright red fire hose, volunteers' drop off point
and notice board.

Built as a place of prayer,
for priests to offer mass, spiritual nourishment,
now criss-crossed by busy feet of vergers,
volunteers, going about their business,
and, at large services, used as a dumping ground
for vestment bags, a robing room.

Cathedral, also built for worship,
for monks to chant, bishops to celebrate,
faithful to receive spiritual nourishment.
Has that now become an empty space,
place of historic interest, tourist trap?
While those responsible for watering flowers,
conducting guided tours, raising the needed funds,
go purposefully about their business utilitarian.

'You shall see angels of God ascending
and descending on the son of man.'
The answer – Incarnation.
Jesus is the place, the meeting place of God and man,
worship and daily life,
communion and collection box,
all meet in him as in this place.

STONE MENAGERIE

A happy horse in desert caravanserai
tasting the grass with relish while
in his master's arms a young man lies supine.
Presumably Sir Edward Coles of this city,
alderman and attorney at law,
is pictured here as Good Samaritan,
his happy-looking horse munching his feed.

Another beast belonging to the Good Samaritan,
with one ear up, the other down,
bites at a dandelion less happily
upon the tomb of Bishop Isaac Maddox of this diocese.

A life-size horse stamps on a fallen eagle
as its rider dies by a musket shot at Waterloo.

Lions and big cats abound,
common as doormats under people's feet.
A cat of sorts, leopard or panther, peeping from folded robe,
lies at the feet of Richard Edes, chaplain to Queen Elizabeth I,
while in the choir a fearsome lion of England
nibbles at King John's sword.
More regal lions surround him
on every side on gaily painted shields.

Two realistic lions guard pulpit steps,
while a more cheerful lion and two beasts
which cannot be identified
rest on two tombs likewise anonymous
and in the north choir aisle two headless lions
rest at the feet of unknown bishop and a knight.

Resting their heads on a black swan apiece,
lie John Beauchamp of Holt and his wife Joan,
greyhound and whippet at their feet as faithful pets.

On the floor two owls keep watch
on Stanley Baldwin's tomb,
while over the west door a ram,
as Abraham raises knife to slay his son,
hides in the bushes, ready for sacrifice.

Ravens abound and eagles.
One lone bird, more raven than a dove,
carries an olive branch
for Alfred Chamberlain Lilly and his wife.

A stone menagerie.
Suppose at night, Cathedral darkened,
moonlight glancing in should wake them all.
What mayhem would ensue,
what roaring, whinnying, barking, hooting cries,
clattering of hooves, the rush of wings,
until the dawning light sends them all back to lie,
silent and still, on tombs of stone.

GOD'S BIG BOOK

'Consider the lilies of the field.'

Matthew 6 v.28

THE ACORN

The green shoot springing from the dark protecting earth
is the first sign we see of life.
We do not see the silent struggle underneath the ground
that hides the winter acorn from our sight.
We do not see the giving up of life,
yielding the substance, shrivelling up the seed,
that searching root and springing shoot
should now have life.
We do not feel the moisture and the bitter cold
causing the shell to crack, then split apart,
the death for life.
For by the time we see the sapling grown
the acorn is no more.
Its life has changed, in form unrecognised,
in substance gone, completely disappeared.

THE TREE

Having ceased
    the sap to rise
    to blossom fair
    ripe fruit to bear
    to offer shade

Only then
    may sun shine through
    to silhouette the tree
    by weather bent
    shaped by its history
    lopped chopped about by man
    toughened by time

Perfect in beauty
    'gainst the evening sky.

THE BIRCH TREE

A birch tree, when 'tis cut,
even the smallest twig, will weep for days.
But those who cut it on their way elsewhere
seldom return to see it weeping still.

'I am the vine', you said, 'and you the branch.
My sap of love flows through me into you.'
Lord, if to make that sap available
to others in their search for you,
I must be cut and wounded, weep for days
tears of your love for them,
teach me to not resent the hurt they do,
nor even to reveal it, lest it mar their quest,
bringing them back again to see me weep.

And if no others here can pray for me,
do you, who stand before the Father's throne,
the Lamb immaculate, plead for me there.
Your prayer sufficient be
for all my needs, to heal my broken heart,
and spread in loving strength to those
for whom I try, inadequate, to pray.

THE 'I' TREE

Strong trunk, enlarged by rings of much experience,
with many fruitful branches; family, friends,
the work I do for you, creative hospitality, walks and leisure.
Fed by communities of faith in which I share,
your word of Jesus, sacrament, quiet times and prayer,
hard times and pain which send the roots down deep,
rocks and blocks round which they work a way,
drawing the nourishment and toughness thence
to nourish, broaden, feed rings of experience.

The season of the year is autumn;
Not sad this fall, but fruitfulness
which can let go of showy leaves, past prime,
to reveal mellow fruit, and seeds of future life.
Weather changeable, basking in sunshine,
tossed about by wind, sparkled by frost and snow.
The soil is rocky, but enriched
by other lives who still feed mine, though theirs are past.
Deep down the water source
which roots seek out in times of dearth and drought.

What sort of tree, dear Lord, am I?
A gnarled oak – still bearing acorns and providing shade.
The branches broken off – my work with lambing,
teaching, rearing children – still useful logs providing warmth.
And, when my life is done, may the trunk provide
materials for other lives to use.

DETAIL

The Malverns in the spring,
when every shade of green
bursts from the earth.
As I walked down the track,
Worcestershire lay
bathed in the sunshine's mirth.

Four cyclists
on their mountain bikes charged past:
'road-holding properties'…
'front wheel or back' was all I heard.
What boring detail!
Hadn't they got eyes?
Or ears to hear a bird?

'Details', I thought,
and how obsessed we are
with details of our lives.
Then, as I looked
at delicate ash leaves
unfurling 'neath the flowers,
I thought of him,
designer of the details of our world,
and none too small to be exact.

We're in his image made,
designed to think in detail, and to speak.
And equally no detail in our lives
too small or boring is
to interest him.

RURAL PENTECOST

Breath of spring on lush green fields
of rippling growing wheat
as rushing wind from heaven
announced the Paraclete.

Candles in horse chestnut trees
glowing fiery red
as tongues of fire alighted
on each apostle's head.

Song of birds from every bush
trilling notes divine
as other tongues sang praises
like those who drink new wine

The summer bursts upon us
out of winter's frost
reminding earth and heaven
of that first Pentecost.

RED

The glossy turning into of the haws
blending yet parting from the green of leaves.
Rich warm and velvety of massive cows
Herefords grazing slow on pastures lush.
Contrast of single brilliancy of poppy
'gainst white and gold backcloth of camomile.
Changingly glorious dazzling dying light
as sun sinks westwards kissing earth goodnight.

All these are red.
Yet as we say the word
we rob them of their glory
deny their colour as we dye our stuff
paint doors and windows
titivate our lips.

The only red, the saving red,
life-giving as 'tis shed, is blood.
Running in rivers from the Saviour's side
dropping in slow gouts from his hands and feet
darkening in beads of sorrow on his brow
mirrored in colour in communion cup
the liquid richness of the grape pressed wine
through which he gives his life for us
once shed in blood.

GREEN SUMMER

Lush hedgerows, full of promise
hazelnuts, unripe, glow pale against the leaves
damsons, hard and dark, in showers hang
as do the ash keys, in a heavy bunch
waiting for autumn winds to waft away.

Perfume pervades the air
from meadowsweet and lady's bedstraw drawn
the honeysuckle clings along the hedge
clover carpeting the grassy verge
busy with bees humming their endless task.

We walk the summer lane,
resting our tired eyes and nerves on hedgerow green,
delight in scent drawn from the flowers bright,
allow the promise of the fruit unseen
to sooth fears, gladden hearts and make us strong.

SUMMER RIVER

Beyond the water gate the river glides,
muddy and flowing fast from last week's rain.
Wednesday it rained for fourteen hours non-stop.

Under the water gate are twenty incised stones;
levels of floods from 1672 until last year,
and all but three were in the winter months.

In winter they hunker down, sandbags at door,
and everything of value moved upstairs.
But now people are jittery because of last week's rain.
Three times, in May, June and July, the water rose.

People in houses fear – this time last year
had to evacuate, now moving back,
wheelbarrow in front window, tables raised.
Barges chug past, skiffs skim the water but, for them,
the river not a pleasure place but whole life's threat.

At Diglis which, last year, was under water,
heavy machinery pounds busily, building more houses.
Are we mad?

THE EDDY
for Mary

The smooth mill stream glides on, an eddy in the midst,
a mini whirlpool, spinning, giddying ring,
endlessly round and round within the flowing stream,
with no way out.

A floating leaf carried upon the stream,
as it floats past, suddenly trapped
within the whirlpool, twisted round and round
for ever seemingly with no way out.
Then just as suddenly it is released,
continues on its way in flowing stream.

I am that leaf borne on life's stream,
then just as suddenly plunged in a whirlpool.
Round and round I go, dizzy and sick
unable to escape or even think,
round and round endlessly with no way out.
Then just as suddenly, when I've lost hope,
I am released, continue in life's stream towards my goal.

Lord, teach me still to trust when in life's stream
I'm sometimes caught,
trapped in the whirlpool of cruel circumstance,
events I can't control, go round and round in panic,
cannot think, let alone trust.
Help me to know I will emerge once more
into life's stream, be carried towards you,
my journey's end.

GARDEN OF DELIGHTS

Each day an empty basket
    with which we enter
        the garden of your delights.

Sometimes it is you
    who gives to us a flower,
        a luscious fruit.
Sometimes the under-gardeners
    load us with vegetables.
Sometimes we pick ourselves
    your bounteous fare.

But sometimes, deliberately or not,
    our basket fills with weeds,
        with heavy stones,
            with slugs and snails.

So at the end of day
    let us unpack
        our basket of delights,
            get rid of weeds,
            enjoy each bloom,
            savour the luscious fruit,
            process the vegetables
            and let them nourish us.
Give thanks for everything.

SHEDDING MY POD

I'm absolutely sure,
when I plant kidney beans,
that they will grow.
I've done it thirty years
with sons and daughters of originals.
They always grow.

I'm just as certain sure,
in fact more so, that Jesus rose.
He said, 'If anyone believes in me,
they'll never die,
but have eternal life.'

I know, of course,
I'll have to shed my pod.
Unwelcome thought.
Shedding my pod,
the bean will still be there,
to grow a resurrection body,
risen in him.

SOLAR FOUNTAIN

Held by a plastic lily pad,
I float on tiny pond,
a square black patch,
with nothing else to do
but soak up sun.

Whenever sun shines through
my batteries recharge
and water, clear and sparkling,
leaps up high,
falls back in glistening drops.

Living water, giving life,
will flow from you, if you believe in me.
So said our Lord.
But often I feel dry, unable to give out.

I need to sit, be still,
do nothing, recharge my batteries,
soak up God's love
and there will flow from me
fountains of glorious life.

FRIENDSHIP

A cat may bear a tortoise company
and be great friends.
Together they may sit and share life's joys,
pooling their wisdom and philosophy.
But if the cat should,
on that friendship's strength,
then wish the tortoise to play cat and mouse,
join in her chase and hunt for birds,
their friendship would be lost.

The cat may wish for tortoise's advice
on how to leap, or when to strike and kill,
but tortoise is unfitted for the chase,
useless in that department to his friend.
He cannot share.
The cat must hunt alone,
nor sharing with a friend, her burden lose
of catching her own prey.

So let the tortoise sweetest friendship share,
companionship, and his just being there,
without demanding that he hunt with you,
which thing by nature he just cannot do.

ATTACHMENT

The feline species is attached
to buildings, has a sense of place.
Cats get upset if forced to move
out of their own accustomed space.

A canine on the other hand
dotes on his master's every word.
He cares not where he is at all
as long as that dear voice is heard.

The Church of England, sad to tell,
has buildings many, people few;
less dogs who love their Master's voice,
more cats who love their favourite pew.

STEPS ON THE PILGRIMAGE

'Let us run with perseverance the race that is set before us.'

Hebrews 12 v.1

DIAKONOS

Unworthy useless tool,
like tiny trowel with which to dig a field,
willing to be God's fool
so that his ground may harvest yield.
              Diakonos.
Heart heavy, sick of prayer,
scared of the thought of years of work to come,
weary, how will I fare
until the end, until the work is done?
              Diakonos.
Mind worried, muddled, dull
and, my thoughts thus, how shall I others teach?
Words stiff and will not flow,
jumbled inside myself, how shall I preach?
              Diakonos.
And sinners, saints, God's flock,
entrusted to my hands, whom I must serve,
who in their needs must mock
my feeble efforts, grieve my every nerve.
              Diakonos.
Another owns the field
and, if a trowel is all he has to dig, then that he'll use,
powerful his hand to wield
the tool I offer, which himself did choose.
              Diakonos.
He too knew what it was
separate from God to feel, and desolate,
as on the cross he hung,
saving the world from its deserved fate.
              Diakonos.
Redemption by the cross;
and so we see God's power in weakness shown,
his kingdom gained by loss,
who, through our service, makes the world his own.
              Diakonos

Written for my husband, Chris, on being ordained deacon
in St Alban's Cathedral 1965

A STONE

Hebrews 2 v.5

A stone
alone
in a field
to trip unwary walkers.
Not much use.

I'd like to stay
alone, quite useless
in my field.
Others deserve to trip
if they disturb me.

A stone
atop a dry stone wall
unshaped
held in by other stones
to mark the bounds
keep stock in, foxes out.
A useful work.

I might not mind
to be atop a wall
if other stones around me
were to fit my awkward shape.
I'd be some use
in marking bounds
and keeping sheep from goats.

A stone
of shining marble
in temple wall
hewn, shaped and chiselled,
polished, cemented in,
immovable
for God's eternal glory
ever used.

I dare not ask
to be a temple stone
hewn from my natural place,
sawn into shape,
odd corners chiselled off,
polished and shining clear,
eternally cemented in by love
with other stones to glorify the Lord.

Yet, Lord, thy kingdom come,
thy will be done.
build with me what you will,
I am your stone.

THOUGHTS ON EPHESIANS 2

What works has he prepared for you today?
You, who in his mercy and his grace,
were brought from death to life.
You, who sit now in heavenly places bright,
adorned in his white robe of righteousness.
For from beginning of created time
he had it in his plan
that you should do some work for him today.

He set the stage,
he placed the actors there,
the prologue and the epilogue are his.
But 'tis your part
to do and say your bit,
the gesture and the line
without which all is incomplete.
He'll be the prompt, and if you are not sure,
he'll give you words to say.
But you must say them. You.
And walk in each good work
he has prepared
for you to do
today.

QUESTIONS OF IDENTITY

'Who are you, Lord, God of our ancestors?
Who shall I say you are?' So Moses asked.
'I AM' was God's reply.

'Who is this man?' disciples cried
when Jesus stilled the storm.
They worshipped him.

'Who are you Lord?'
questioned the blinded Saul
on the Damascus road.
'I am Jesus, the one you persecute,'
was the reply.

Who do I think I am?
Beloved child of God,
dead, raised in him
who gave himself for me,
living with him in life eternally.

I AM

I AM who I AM
the same,
yesterday, today, for ever,
was, am, will be.

I AM calls me to BE
a human BEING not a human DOING
unique individual, not defined
by ancestors, place or experience
but as a twinkle in God's eye
before creation,
BEING now to all eternity.

WHO DO YOU THINK YOU ARE?

My parents' daughter,
then for many years the vicar's wife,
my daughters' Mum and now their children's Granny.
Do I define myself totally in terms of next of kin;
my parents, husband, offspring?

Who do I think I am?
Only a brief few years, two, three at college
between my parents' home
and looking forward to my married state.

Who do you think you are?
When faced with that, no wonder I have fears
of utter worthlessness in my own self.
Prone to depression, I am wont to cry,
'You'd all be better off without me here.'

Who do I think I am?
Once in my teens
I heard the Lord's voice calling, 'Joan', my name.
I know that I am 'Joan' and what 'Joan' means;
'The gift of God.'
God doesn't give bad gifts.
I am his gift to those I meet,
to those for whom I'm daughter, wife and mother.

Who do you think you are?
Paul asked, 'Who are you, Lord?' on the Damascus road.
You answered, 'I am Jesus' and in working out
the implications of that simple word,
Paul found himself.

Who do I think I am?
I was a twinkle in God's loving eye before creation was;
of so much worth that, for my sake,
he sent his Son to live and die upon the cross
and rise again,
that I might live in him for all eternity,

Who do I think I am?
I am a child of God.
In finding him I lose myself and rise again in him,
a new creation; Joan, his precious gift.
That's who I am.

INTO HIS ARMS

'Welcome' it says, and 'Please come in'.
I'm sure that can't refer to me.
I don't want to disturb you, Lord,
or be a nuisance to you now.
That's what I'm sure I'd be.

I'll just creep in around the door
and stay here, hidden, out of sight.
To be with you in this still room
is quite enough for now.
I'd rather not come out into the light.

Your name means 'Gift of God'.
What kind of gift do you give to your friends?
Something you'd love to have yourself,
a precious, valued, treasured find.
That's the kind of gift God sends.

So come into the light my child,
where I can see you and enjoy
the gift that I have made
and cleansed and treasured.
Be sure that you will not annoy.

Come closer still,
right up to me
stretch out your hand to touch.
Then I'll stoop down to gather you
into my arms upon my knee,
that I may love you much.

I hear your heart beneath me beat,
accepted, loved and all forgiven,
I snuggle up, I am at rest,
safe in my loving Father's arms,
and that shall be my heaven.

COME

I'm miserable. I'm in a mess.
I'm really in the pit.
I'm feeling sorry for myself.
I really do not fit.
And no one noticed how I feel,
enquiring tenderly.
I've been a pain so long I s'pose,
they've now just ceased to see.

Sheer misery.
Then as I plumb the depths
I see you standing Lord,
smiling, with arms outstretched.
You enquire tenderly,
'Why are you standing over there
when you could come to me?'

At your command I come, O Lord,
like Peter, from the boat.
Walking above the depths of pain
and misery, I float.
My peace returns, the depths recede,
and I am saved from harm.
You hold me in you arms, dear Lord,
I'm loved and all is calm.

DEPRESSION or SODDEN SPRING

'The rain continued forty nights and days.' So Scripture says.
For forty days this spring we have had rain and bitter cold.
Not continuous, true, but every day we have had rain.

The heavy clouds drop rain day in, day out, with no relief.
The fields lie sodden. Waiting for the rain, we cannot plant.
The gardens, pudding-like, sprout nought but weeds we cannot pull.

My tears and wallowing turned fertile ground into a bog.
Despair laid low the eager springing grass. It cannot rise.
Too many tears, too many blameful sins, all round is mire.

Lord, let your sun shine on your servants here to dry the mud,
to draw the moisture from the sullen ground, warming the earth,
that both the fields and gardens, and my soul, may harvest yield.

FORGIVENESS

We must not keep account, as Peter tried, to equal sins
that we forgive with those we'll be forgiven.
The judgement that we pass on others will be that
by which we will ourselves by God be measured.

Rather, as we ask forgiveness for those sins which we,
through weakness, negligence or quite deliberate fault, have done,
and understand the damage done to us, in childhood,
or by others' thoughtless words, which caused us so to act,

so we shall understand that wrongs done and received by us
or others are so caused by other damaged folk,
and our forgiveness will flow out to them in understanding and in gratitude
that all before our our loving and good God are sinners – but forgiven.

GUIDANCE

When I hear your voice on the lips of Christian friends
or from strangers met by chance, then I bless you, Lord.
Help me as they speak to pay attention to you, Lord,
to hear your word and understand and obey you, Lord.

When I read your word and see you working in the past
with people, things and history, help me to see you, Lord,
patterns of your care and promises made long ago
are still for me to know your love and obey you, Lord.

When there is a mess in the circumstance of life
and I don't know which way to turn, help me to trust you, Lord.
Let me see your hand in things that happen and in change
that you provide a way for me to obey you, Lord.

When I pray alone in my trysting place with you,
quiet my heart and still my mind till I hear you, Lord.
Give my heart your peace in decisions that I make
that I may know your guiding hand and obey you, Lord

THE TELEPHONE

Brrr…Brrr   Brrr…Brrr
The ring tones sound, demanding a response,
demanding that I pick up the receiver,
demanding that I speak and ask 'Who's there?'
demanding that I listen to the other voice.

And if I do not answer,
it will go on ringing for a while
and then will stop.

Your ring tones sound, dear Lord,
around us all the time;
the beauty of a sunset, cry of need,
whisper of conscience, other people's eyes.
Your phone rings, Lord, demanding a response,
demanding that I pick up the receiver,
ask 'Who's there?' and listen to your voice.

And if I do not answer,
it will go on ringing for a while
and then will stop.
And I will never know
what word you had for me.

OASIS

See the pool of cooling water,
stood about with tall palm trees,
all around, the scorching desert,
unrefreshed by shade or breeze.

Still the pool lies, cool and silent,
ever filled from depths below.
Here can come the weary travellers,
peace and sweet refreshment know.

Here they taste of living water,
quench their thirst and drink their fill.
Here no mirage, ever moving
but a pool for ever still.

So shall you be that oasis,
patient, on your bed of pain,
that all those who seek your presence
may their calm and peace regain.

Weary from the world's long struggle,
hurry, bustle, here and there,
they will come to you for succour,
strengthened by your love and care.

Only by your silent struggle
coping with your pain and loss
can you draw the living waters
he released upon the cross

As you drink his living water,
from your depths shall waters flow,
strengthening the weary pilgrims
more than ever you will know.

THE SOAKAWAY

Communication does not have to be
expressed in words: I soak up
what other people feel,
their fears and burdens, tension, anger, sorrow.
It drains me dry, exhausting body, mind and soul.
I need to turn into a soakaway.
Water, drained through the soil,
the humus, root of the word humility,
is cleansed and purified.
Then I too need to be drenched through
with your life-giving water from the spring
of your eternal life.
Lord, give me humility to be your soakaway.

HOLDING THE SPONGE

Lord, you have given us a ministry –
holding the sponge;
being there and listening,
absorbing all the aggro, sorrow, pain,
until the sponge is soaked.

Our mistake, dear Lord,
was not to wring it out,
let you soak up, absorb,
the contents of the sponge,
relieve us of its weight,
return it to us light and dry,
ready for use again.

Be with us as we learn to hold the sponge,
absorb the troubles and then wring them out
into your ever open heart and start again.

POOL OF TEARS

Every so often in my pilgrimage
I come across a pool of tears.

Pool of my tears;
deep sorrow, loss and grief,
sad tears, tears of release,
salt healing tears, tears of relief,
filling the pool and welling up again
in tears of joy.

And then a pool of penitential tears;
tears such as Peter wept
when he denied his Lord;
tears of the woman washing Jesus' feet,
wiping them with her hair;
tears leading to forgiveness, life restored
to love, follow and serve the risen Lord.

Then, deepest pool of all,
your tears, dear Lord;
such as you wept over Jerusalem,
longing to draw her children to yourself;
or at the grave of Lazarus, your friend,
sharing the bitterness of our humanity;
that is the healing pool of tears indeed,
Immanuel, God with us, weeps with us
in that pool of your tears.

SUNDAY WORSHIP

From rocky mountain heights and towering crags
trickles of water, widening rivulets
join peat stained sluggish seeping from the bogs.
Each current, bearing its own history,
enters the lake.

So we, from far and near, in cars, by wheelchair, bike,
hobbling on sticks, brisk walking through the streets,
each bringing our own lives,
our worries, relatives, friends and concerns,
gather in church.

The lake consumes the streams, joins them in one.
They, entering its depths, are stilled,
and so reflect the sun, the mountain scene,
as rippling streams can never do.

The liturgy enfolds us in its depths,
enriched by ages, spirit-stilling, peace,
as God shines on his church
and we respond in worship,
reflecting back his glorious beauty, life.

The streams disperse again,
not in disordered, tumbling rivulets
but irrigation channels,
each directed to thirsty crops and fields.

So we, enriched by worship, are sent forth
into the channels he's prepared for us,
to spread his life and light
into a needy world.

UNITY

On the snooker table in the frame,
a perfect triangle, hard shining balls,
a patterned unity.
Then click! crash! wham!
Spectacular as ball strikes ball;
kisses and cannons at a tangent fly,
knocking each other into the right place
to win the game.
The balls stay all unmarked, shining and hard.

       A sandy hummock in a field,
       a slatted wooden hive;
       nothing much to show.
       Observe more closely though, and you will find
       a living, but untidy, unity.
       The ant-hill and the hive of bees;
       busy, busy every one,
       each knowing their own place, their special task.
       A common purpose, passed on through a chain
       far more effective than our best pcs:
       Instant communication to the whole.

And we, our church, our Christian fellowship?
Are we the snooker balls,
gathered in tidy pattern once a week,
then knocked, dispersed,
moving each other, being moved,
but never really touched, or marked, or wounded
through our hard shell?

       Or are we like the insects; ant-hill, hive,
       untidy unity, living together,
       knowing our right place, our function,
       with a common aim
       communicated by the Spirit of our God?
          Like oil on Aaron's beard,
          Glorious and messy,
          Permeating all,
          Lived unity.

THE DANCE

At first I danced for joy. My heart was free.
I danced along the beach, beside the sea,
each move and step and turn chosen for me.
I danced for joy.

Then took I you for Dancing Master, Lord,
Attended to instructions, every word.
Concentrated. Left, backward, forward, right.
I danced for you.

As I became accustomed, following you,
the steps were easier. I found I could do
dance without thinking. Dance with others too.
I'd learned to dance.

But harder dances, more complex, you taught.
Painful the steps, almost a battle fought,
resisting pressure to step where I ought.
Dancing was hard.

Now I relax, dear Lord, in your embrace,
looking not at your feet, but at your face,
matching my steps to yours, and to your pace,
I dance with you.

So, Lord, you are the dance. You set me free
always and evermore to dance with thee,
until in effortless accord join we
the dance eternal.

THE OFFERING
These are the offerings to lay on his shrine.

I struggle, Lord, to render it to you,
that offering, such a little thing,
yet so great in my eyes.
I wrench it from me,
lay it grudgingly upon your altar stone.
Look how it lies there,
small, the tiniest token, hardly to be seen,
of all the gifts that you have given me.

Yet you accept joyfully,
gladly and with gratitude,
not just that gift, but its heart value.
All the cost to me you take unto yourself,
endow it with such value as I thought it had.
So when I reach that place where I can see
how paltry was the gift I offered thee,
then you will give it back, all glorified,
precious as if I died to give it thee.

ON THE RAILS
Going into retreat

So many words, Lord. Impossible to worship.
Words of Scripture rolling over me.
Words of choruses battering my ears.
What am I doing? Not worshipping?

Then I see:

Arriving at the station, preparing to board the train,
I look round at my fellow travellers,
in the bookshop gather material
for thought and reading on the journey.
I find the platform, board the train,
select my seat, facing the right way
in order to see the view; no blockages to sight.
A table is a must, on which to read, to write,
and place the coffee with which I am supplied.

All ready now, every need satisfied,
and mind at rest, attentive now, my Lord,
to concentrate on where you're taking me,
the beauty I will see along the way,
until with you I reach the end
and see you face to face.

RETREAT

The following four poems were written during a retreat, and used to lead others.

REST

It's all right now, everything's all right,
you're quite safe here with me.
I've brought you right away,
beyond the enemy fire, out of his reach,
so that you may rest.
Yes, rest.

I know it's hard.
You're shell-shocked, nerves on edge.
You jump at every noise.
So used to being on your guard,
tense, ready to defend yourself, attack.
Now you must rest.
Yes, rest.

Of course you cannot sleep.
Your mind won't stop.
What's the foe up to now?
Where's the next strike?
Will the line hold?
Or will the ammunition all run out?
Now leave the worrying to me,
for you must rest.
Yes, rest.

Here on a little grassy patch of land,
beneath the oak tree's shade,
watching the mountain stream
and listening to its unending song.
Let your eyes rest on ripples over rocks,
let your ears rest in soothing constant sound,
let body rest on yielding sunlit turf,
so mind will rest.
Yes, rest
in my own presence safe.

HEALING

You have first aid whilst on the battle line
to staunch the flow of blood, and keep you fighting.
But when you have retreated, then's the time
for wounds to be uncovered, lay them bare,
to let the surgeon do his healing work,
ease out the pus, excise the festering sores,
extract the shrapnel, close the bullet holes,
pour in the salve, transfuse life-giving blood.
Then rest you till your wounds are healed,
completely, wholly, not even a twinge,
to bring back memories of ancient hurts.
For he will make you whole, to fight again.

REPLENISH SUPPLIES

Am I to see the picnic all set out
and have no part in it myself?
Jesus, I see you spread the tablecloth,
placing upon it bread and cup of wine.
You wait, inviting, for us all to sit,
then take the Bread of Life and break it there.
You give it us, and then the cup, to share
in memory of you.

Dear Lord, I take the bread and drink the cup.
It strengthens me for battles still ahead,
I know, but still I cannot taste a thing.
Eating's no fun, sweet Lord, when I've a cold.
I do it just to stay the hunger pangs.
I drink to slake my thirst,
but whether it be wine or blood I cannot tell.

Lord, weary from battle do I sit me down.
The feast you have prepared:
The wine, the bread, the Paschal lamb, the bitter herbs,
and sweetest fruit of Paradise itself.
I eat, Lord, as you have commanded me,
and know that in the strength of bread you give
I can go on anew,
out into the battle once again,
as once Elijah went
for forty days into the wilderness
in strength of bread which you provided him.

And yet, O Lord, I long to taste you now,
your goodness and your sweet delight.
Weary I am, though ought I not to say,
of walking still by faith and not by sight.

SHARPEN AND REPAIR WEAPONS

Our weapons need renewing by you, Lord.
The truth gets bent, our righteousness is soiled,
battered our faith, and quenched our fiery sword,
the power divine grows weak, our prayer is spoiled.

You may disarm us, Lord, while here we rest,
take all our war-stained armour to renew.
Here is no enemy to put us to the test.
Our armour then return, renewed by you.

For it is your salvation that we wear,
your righteousness protects, your Word we wield,
shod with your Gospel, joined to you by prayer,
guided by you, the Truth, your faith our shield.

We kneel before you, Lord, in homage due,
receiving back our armour at your hand,
praying that we may use it all for you,
until we're glory-crowned in Promised Land.

PRAYER BEFORE SLEEP

No, I am not afraid of the dark,
of ghoulies and ghosties and three legged beasties
and things that go bump in the night.

I love the night sky,
being abroad in darkness,
dim silhouettes of branches,
twigs snapping underfoot.

'And if I die before I wake,
I pray the Lord my soul to take.'
That is my fear; disintegration,
losing my self, my reason,
unable to control my thoughts,
reactions, make chaos orderly,
connected, understood,
losing my mind.

That's what I fear.

Prayer of a child, unrecognised,
lifelong insomnia,
unable to let go.

'Into thy hands, O Lord.'

THE RESERVOIR

All the springs of mercy are dried up in me,
cracked like a potsherd,
dried up reservoir in drawn out drought,
crazed pattern of deep chasms in hard baked clay.
My Lord, I thirst.

The first rains come, spots here and there,
marking the sun baked clay, then disappear.
What good was that?

Long drawn out drizzling mist
softens the outline of the jagged cracks,
darkens the clay, begins to run together,
glisten, shine. It's empty still, but wet.
Perhaps a tiny trickle of a stream
creeps in the higher end, then disappears.
When will it fill again, O Lord, how long?

You showed me, as I stood at Jenny's Leap,
the ocean, limitless, and rushing clouds.
There's water there, enough for everything.
But I must wait;
Give time, take time, for ocean to evaporate,
moisture drawn up to form the clouds above,
to drop their rain upon my reservoir.

Now it is raining hard,
the muddy floor is filling up, mountain stream pouring in.
And as the rain soaks all the moorland grass
the moisture trickles through,
forms myriad streams which flow
into the reservoir all round the edge.

'Soon there will be enough for you to give.
When you give now, you give of sparse resource,
and emptied are, dried up again.
But then, when you have given time
for me to fill your reservoir,
love will flow out again from hidden depths.
You must be hollowed out.'
'Oh no, Lord, no, not like a hollow tree.'
'No, like a lake which, as the currents flow,
the depths are scoured to hold more water,
fresh and cool. flowing and strong and free.'

And finally I saw only a thin divide,
a strip of land keeping me from the sea,
and when you break that down, or wear it through,
the lake becomes a fjord, still and deep,
united now for ever with the sea,
the everlasting ocean of your love.

NEW CHAPTER 2008

So now a chapter ends.
A full ten years of doings laid aside and passed to you:
trainer of Readers, tutor for St John's and LMTs,
leader of worship and prayer counsellor,
editor, proofreader and trustee,
the vicar's wife, leader of prayer and study groups,
shepherd's assistant during lambing time.
All these I give to you with heartfelt thanks
for using talents given by you to touch so many lives,
sometimes so deeply, with your love and grace.
Thanks that they saw in me your love and care
as I am being changed into your likeness, Lord.
Take these ten years, completed chapter,
handed now to you to edit, proofread,
correct mistakes, blot out my sins,
and store it in your treasury
until the final chapter ends,
the book is closed.
    I offer to you now a new blank page,
    next chapter of my life.
    Being, not doing is, I think, the theme.
    Being for you. The Jesus Prayer,
    and intercession ceaselessly with thanks,
    rejoicing constantly.
        Being for Chris
        facing together adventure of old age,
        increasing frailty of body, mind,
        holding each other up,
        encouraging in fears, hopes, joys and daily life.
            Being for family
            daughters and sons-in-law, grandchildren,
            bringing joy and challenge and their love.
                Being for friends
                as they, too, face old age, illness and death,
                holding them in the hope of your eternity.
Until the final chapter ends, the book is closed.
Author and completer of my life,
thanks be to you.

SAINT JOAN AT THE STAKE

Hands pinned behind my back.
'Hail Mary, full of grace…
in the hour of death pray for me now.'

Kindling beneath my feet.
'Sweet saints who spoke to me
where are you now?'

All eyes on me, on me alone,
gloating, expecting… what?
'Lord Jesus, Son of God,
have mercy now.'

The smell of burning pitch
strikes at my nostrils.
'Will you recant?'
'No! No! and No!'

Fire kindles now.
'Father into thy hands…
Fear, pain resolved, to you I fly.'

FIFTY GOLDEN YEARS

Early years flecks of gold from lumps of ore
unearthed in Kent's gold hopyards,
college years, our marriage, birth of Alison.
The hard rock smashed away
by the adversity of breakdown,
being out of work, the endless search for jobs.
Gold further sifted out and gathered up at Droitwich,
births of Clare and Rachel,
holiday in Wales which led us to our cottage.
Dross worn away in mental hospital,
further depression, work relationships.
Difficult decision moving to Birmingham.
There in the melting pot of desperate needs
the Holy Spirit turned our gold
into a radiant stream of God's great love
for those who needed it on the estates.
More dross burned out by illness, hospital and disability.
The crucible of Tyseley, Lucy's arrival, inner city life.
Being misunderstood, yet all the while
aware of God transforming people's lives
and shining through the dark.
Another move to Holt, further refining,
moulding into shape by study, parish ministry,
the wider diocese and children leaving home.
Last parish in the Forest moulded us further,
being part of small communities,
and at the House of Bread
burnishing the gold, removing blemishes.

Now in retirement thankfully still together
polished in one mirror reflecting the love of God.
Help us to keep the mirror bright,
less doing and more being
as we wait together for that final consummation
when we shall be pure gold in God our sun.

INDEX of TITLES and First lines